Lewis
and
the First Day
Jitters

Written by Colleen Grove

Illustrated by Manas Dash

ISBN: 978-1-7781146-3-2 (Paperback)

For Lewis. You're going to rock it in kindergarten.
I love you my sweet boy. You've got this!

Lewis was nervous for his first day of school,

Even though taking a school bus sounded pretty cool.

His tummy was full of butterflies and his hands clammy too,

Because new things are scary, exciting, and nerve wracking too.

He could see the school bus coming down the road,

But how would he know where to sit without being told?

Luckily, the bus driver was kind and showed him where to go,

So he took his seat and decided to go with the flow.

Lewis was confused there were no seatbelts anywhere,

But remembered Mommy told him that while she helped him prepare.

So he knew he was safe and he'd gotten past the first scary step,

And at the next stop was his friend Sheila! That gave him some pep!

Seeing Sheila made him feel better and he knew he wasn't alone,

She was nervous too, but having a friend there helped set the tone.

Hand in hand, they watched more and more kids get on the bus,

And they all got on without much of a fuss!

Next thing they knew, they were arriving at school,

It's so big and exciting and scary and cool!

They felt like big kids on an adventure now,

There were big kids and little kids everywhere! Wow!

SCHOOL

Lewis took it all in as he looked around,

Then uncertainty took over and on his face was a frown.

How would he know what to do and where to go,

He chewed on his collar and exhaled with a big blow.

Suddenly, there was Rowan, his very best friend!

Saying, "Come on Lewis, this way, our classroom's at the end!"

Lewis felt so relieved, he chased Rowan down the hall,

Then he got this wonderful feeling that kindergarten will be a ball!

Their teacher greeted them at the door,

She was so nice and kind, it made Lewis want to see more!

He spent the day learning, playing, and having fun,

He was actually sad when it was time for the day to be done.

Good Morning Class
CLASS

Back on the bus and back home he went,

Lewis couldn't wait to tell his parents how his day was spent.

When he got off the bus, he had a huge smile on his face,

He ran into his mom's arms and gave her a big embrace!

Lewis told her everything about his first day at school,

And was no longer nervous because school really rules!

He walked in the house and put down his backpack,

And Lewis couldn't wait until he could go back!

Visit my website:
https://www.colleengrovechildrensauthor.ca
OR
Facebook @
https://www.facebook.com/colleengroveauthor
OR
Instagram @
https://www.instagram.com/colleengrovechildrensauthor

About the Author:

Colleen Grove lives on an acreage near Stony Plain, Alberta with her husband and two young children. She has degrees in psychology and education and has always worked with children and families in some capacity. This is Colleen's second book and was inspired to write this story because her son is entering kindergarten this year and has been struggling with a mix of excitement and nervousness.

Colleen is also the author of Malcolm and The FunKey Monkey: The Magic Key. The second book in this series is coming soon...stay tuned!